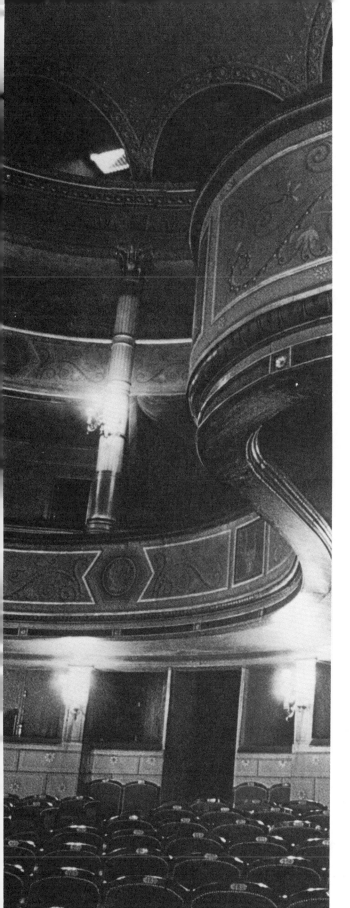

Romantic concert hall at the Conservatory of Music, Paris (see page 4).

Second Edition
Copyright © MCMXCII by Alfred Publishing Co., Inc.

THE RO...

An Introduction to the Piano Music

Edited by
Willard A. Palmer & Margery Halford

Contents

FOREWORD 2
> The Romantic Era 2; The Spirit of Romanticism 2; The Piano and Its Contributions 3; A Romantic Setting for Romantic Performances 4; Ornamentation 5; Problems in Rhythmic Notation 6; About Pedaling 6; About Tempo Rubato 7.

WEBER, SCHUBERT, & BEETHOVEN 8
Air & Variation — C. M. von Weber 10
Waltz in B Minor — Franz Schubert 14
Scherzo in B-flat Major — Franz Schubert 16
Sonata quasi una Fantasia — Ludwig van Beethoven 20

JOHN FIELD 24
Nocturne No. 5 — John Field 24

MENDELSSOHN, SCHUMANN, & CHOPIN 28
Venetian Gondola Song No. 2 — Felix Mendelssohn 30
Consolation — Felix Mendelssohn 32
Reverie — Robert Schumann 34
The Wayside Inn — Robert Schumann 36
Important Event — Robert Schumann 39
Waltz in A-flat Major — Frederic Chopin 40
Nocturne in C Minor — Frederic Chopin 44

EDVARD GRIEG 48
Waltz in A Minor — Edvard Grieg 48
Arietta — Edvard Grieg 52

LISZT, BRAHMS, & OTHERS 54
Adagio in E Major — Franz Liszt 56
Etude in C Major — Franz Liszt 58
Waltz in C-sharp Minor — Johannes Brahms 61
Intermezzo in A Minor — Johannes Brahms 62

TEACHERS:
SEE THE IMPORTANT NOTE ON PAGE 7!

Cover painting by Fitz Hugh Lane
Boston Harbor, Sunset
Oil on canvas, 1850-55
The Granger Collection, New York

The Romantic Era

Emotional

Sensitive

Poetic

Dreamy

Vague

Melancholy

Yearning

Sentimental

Romantic portrait of Johann Wolfgang Goethe, whose poems inspired Beethoven, Schubert, and many others.

Fantastic

Dramatic

Flamboyant

Heroic

Tragic

Intense

Tempestuous

Colossal

The words on each side of the picture describe the two distinct but complementary types of romantic music: the small and lyrical, and the huge and dramatic.

The composer no longer expected the performer to be his co-creator and to exercise his own "good taste" in interpreting the music, as in the baroque era.

The classical era, in which many important details of performance were still entrusted to the performer, had given way to an age in which the composer was very explicit in his instructions, using all manner of descriptive words and symbols to indicate exactly how the music should be played.

THE SPIRIT OF ROMANTICISM

In an age when the common man became recognized as an individual with emotions and needs of his own, it was natural that music and other art forms would begin to break away from the restrained, balanced elegance of the classical era. In the painting of the poet Goethe (above), clearly romantic characteristics are shown in the wind-swept hair, the casually wrapped garments with the hand clasping them around his shoulders, and in the vague, shadowy figures behind him. Formal balance and

symmetry have no place in this painting. Its purpose is to illuminate the poetic nature of the man.

Composers reacted to the new freedom and emotionalism of the age by creating new forms for their compositions and by going beyond the limits of the already-existing forms. The new forms reflected every man's most personal emotions and his longing for the beautiful and the truly unattainable. Those who wrote strongly nationalistic music appealed to the deeply rooted patriotism which every man cherished. The listener could weep or cheer or exult or pine sentimentally with the composer, and his favorite dreams could be harmlessly indulged in fantasy as the music engulfed him. No longer under the patronage of either the court or church, the composer became an important element of the social world, both as performer at concerts and as honored guest in fashionable homes.

As the composer was expressing his own personal emotions in his works, he left less and less to the discretion of the performer. Ornaments were more often than not incorporated in the melodic line, instead of being written as symbols, and minute directions for performance tempo, dynamics, phrasing, and style were written on the music score.

THE PIANO AND ITS CONTRIBUTIONS

Ornate grand piano by Erard, built around 1830.

The piano was the perfect instrument for romanticism. It already had the ability to produce a wide range of volume, but as the frame was strengthened, the hammers made larger and heavier, and the strings placed under greater tension, it became a thundering giant, capable of expressing the most violent raging. Because of the infinite control of touch that it now possessed, the piano could also express the tenderest and most delicate sentimentalism, gradually reducing its volume to caressing *pianissimos*. The damper pedal helped to influence composers to write long, legato melodies, and the slur began to take on its modern meaning of *legato*. No matter how widely spaced the melody and harmony or how intricate the movement of each part, they could all be blended with the damper pedal into a richly harmonic fabric that ideally suited the new chromatic chord progressions the romantic composers used so freely.

At concerts the piano was turned sideways so that the performer's profile could be seen and the audience could watch his hands. It was during the romantic era that the solo concert began, and the performer became a hero to his audience. Here was the opportunity for the artist to display the full range of his technical and interpretive abilities. Virtuosity reached almost unbelievable heights.

As soon as the upright piano was developed, it became an instant favorite, and nearly every home had one. Transcriptions of orchestral and ensemble works were printed almost before the premier performance was heard, and composers wrote short, lyrical pieces with modest technical demands to meet the growing need for emotionally appealing music that everyone could learn to play. Publishers produced what Berlioz called "an avalanche of romances, a torrent of airs and variations," to supply the insatiable demand.

Pleyel upright piano with decorative handles and inlays, and built-in candelabra.

3

The piano became the center of entertainment in the home. The family gathered around the instrument in the evening to listen and to sing. The *soirée*, to which guests were invited for musical entertainment, became one of the most popular forms of recreation.

Pianos poured from hundreds of factories, extravagantly gilded and decorated, and built in various fantastic shapes, with features such as built-in candelabra, sliding racks that could be pulled out for holding candles or lamps, ornate handles for moving the instruments, or as many as eight pedals for producing various novel effects, etc. One of the first upright pianos, built by Broadwood of London (see picture), housed the vertical strings in a curtained case almost nine feet tall. This top-heavy construction was soon abandoned for the design more similar to the modern upright.

Upright piano by Broadwood.

Concert hall at the Conservatory of Music, Paris.

A ROMANTIC SETTING FOR ROMANTIC PERFORMANCES

Grandiose concert halls, such as the one pictured at the left, provided appropriate settings for romantic operas, which were presented with extravagant costumes and no small amount of melodrama. Here Franz Liszt, Anton Rubinstein, Sigismund Thalberg, and dozens of other virtuosos dazzled audiences with their pianistic fireworks. In this auditorium, the super-violinist Niccolò Paganini played with such incredible skill that many of his amazed listeners believed he was in league with the devil. In the same hall, Hector Berlioz' *Fantastic Symphony* had its first performance. Paganini was so overwhelmed by this symphony, that he made Berlioz a gift of 20,000 francs (about $4,000) as a token of his esteem.

ORNAMENTATION

In 1828, Johann Nepomuk Hummel, a brilliant concert pianist who was a pupil of Mozart, wrote an important method book for piano, which became widely used. In the book he proposed that trills be played beginning with the principal note rather than the upper auxiliary. Chief among his reasons was that the melody is more apparent when the trill begins on the melody note. He acknowledged that until 1828, when his book was published, trills were generally begun on the upper auxiliary, and it is important to note that Weber died in 1826, Beethoven in 1827, and Schubert in 1828. So we may be sure that Hummel's decision did not affect the way their trills were played. We may believe that these composers were in agreement with Clementi's practices, which stated that trills generally begin on the upper note, but that trills following stepwise motion in a legato melody, or very short trills on passing tones, could begin on the principal note.

Not all composers immediately accepted Hummel's proposal, and among those who did not was Frederic Chopin, who, according to his pupils, generally began his trills on the upper note. Since Chopin used Clementi's books, we may believe that the exceptions he allowed were those listed by Clementi.

1. THE APPOGGIATURA ♪ ♪

The long appoggiatura is generally written out in large notes in music of the romantic era.

The short appoggiatura, usually written as a small 16th note (♬ or ♪), is played very quickly, on the beat of the principal note. Sometimes it is played almost simultaneously with the principal note.

2. THE TURN ∾

When the turn appears over the note, it begins immediately, on the upper auxiliary, on the beat of the principal note.

When the turn appears after the note, the principal note is played before the turn is begun.

3. THE TRILL IN MUSIC OF WEBER, SCHUBERT, BEETHOVEN, FIELD AND CHOPIN

The trill generally begins on the upper auxiliary. A termination is usually added, whether indicated or not.

The trill need not be precisely measured. It may begin slowly and increase in speed.

When the trill is played legato with the preceding upper or lower 2nd, it may begin on the principal note.

A small note on the same line or space as the trilled note indicates that the trill begins on that note (the principal note).

The sign ᷉ is frequently used to indicate a short trill, beginning on the upper auxiliary.

The sign ᷉ may also indicate a passing or transient trill, especially in rapid, descending passages.

4. THE TRILL IN MUSIC OF MENDELSSOHN, SCHUMANN, GRIEG, LISZT AND BRAHMS

The trill generally begins on the principal note. A termination is usually added, whether indicated or not.

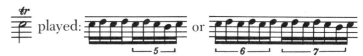

The trill need not be precisely measured. It may begin slowly and increase in speed.

A small note on the line or space a 2nd higher than the trilled note indicates that the trill begins on that note (the upper auxiliary).

The sign ᷉ indicates a *passing* or *transient trill*.

5. THE MORDENT

The mordent disappeared from general use in the music of the romantic period.

PROBLEMS IN RHYTHMIC NOTATION

In the baroque and classical eras, two equally notated 8th notes were often played *unequally*, especially when they occurred together with triplets in another voice:

This is called "accommodated rhythm."

Dotted rhythms were often similarly accommodated when they occurred simultaneously with triplet rhythms:

The reason for this was that the modern custom of writing a triplet containing only TWO NOTES (as in the 2nd part of each of the above examples) had not yet been adopted.

During the late years of the classical era and through the romantic era, however, the appearance of the music page was beginning to change. Composers were writing out ornaments, more slurs, dynamics, tempo directions, and indications for pedaling. It became necessary to be more exact in notating rhythms, so that ♩. ♪ would not mistakenly be played ♩ 3 ♪. One of the early ways of showing how the rhythm should be played occurs in measure 3 of the Weber *Variation* on page 12. The eighth notes in the treble staff have their stems joined with the triplets, to show the notes that are played at the same time. The eighth notes in the bass must, of course, be similarly accommodated.

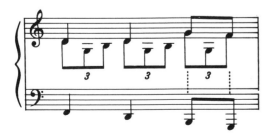

In the Beethoven *Sonata* on pages 20-24, however, the dotted rhythms occurring against triplets are not accommodated. Czerny, who studied with Beethoven, said that the 16th notes in measure 5 and similar places must be struck *after* the last note of the triplet, and that the triplets must be played throughout with perfect equality.

Other instances of both the old and new types of notation may be found until very late in the romantic era, when the exact notation of triplets had become completely accepted by all composers.

ABOUT PEDALING

The direction *senza sordino*, used by Beethoven in his *Sonata quasi una Fantasia*, Op. 27, No. 1 (page 20), has proved confusing to some pianists. An explanation follows:

When the damper pedal is depressed, it lifts each damper (called *sordino* in Italian) off the strings, making the sounds continue. Thus the direction *senza sordino* ("without damper") means to USE the pedal, removing the dampers from the strings. According to Czerny, who was Beethoven's pupil, the pedal should be lifted and depressed again each time the bass note changes. If Beethoven intended the pedal to be held down throughout the movement, it was because his piano had less resonance and sustaining power than modern instruments, and the effect would certainly be different from that on the modern piano.

Romantic composers used the symbols 𝄆. ✳ to indicate the application and release of the pedal. These markings are not as precise as the modern ⌞_____⌟ , and with them it is not as easy to show when the pedal is released and depressed on the same note (⌞____⋀____⌟). In this book the more recently developed system is used. In old-music, the so-called rhythmic pedaling (⌞____⌟ ⌞____⌟) is often replaced by "overlapping" pedaling (⌞____⋀____⌟) by modern performers.

ABOUT *TEMPO RUBATO*

Tempo rubato, literally "robbed time," is a device that was used frequently by pianists of the romantic era, especially Field, Chopin and Liszt. In earlier periods this practice is also mentioned, notably by C. P. E. Bach and by Mozart, who wrote, in a letter to his father, "These people cannot grasp that in *tempo rubato* the right hand goes its way, while the left hand plays in strict time."

Some have incorrectly regarded *tempo rubato* as the alteration of tempo by slowing and then moving faster, to emphasize certain musical effects. But as Mozart notes above — and this is confirmed by Chopin and Liszt — the accompaniment does not vary in tempo. Thus in a true rubato, the melody may be played a bit "out of time" with the accompaniment, now leading, now following it. In this type of rubato the hands, then, are not played precisely together as the music indicates, but the melody is performed somewhat freely around a steadily moving accompaniment. Needless to say, it should not be overdone, nor used in brilliant, fiery passages.

Tempo rubato is sometimes indicated by the composer, but it was freely employed by romantic pianists whenever they pleased. It should be used in the two Chopin selections in this book (pp. 40-47), as well as the *Adagio* by Liszt (p. 56).

NOTE TO TEACHERS

The pieces in this book are arranged in chronological order, to properly illustrate the development of music during the romantic era. The printed material should be carefully studied in the order presented, but the pieces may be studied in whatever order the teacher judges to be in the best interest of the student.

ACKNOWLEDGMENTS

The editors wish to express their gratitude for the assistance of the many people who have contributed their time, special skills, and painstaking attention to the preparation of this book. To the following go our special thanks:

To Judith Linder, our brilliant assistant, whose knowledge and expertise are reflected in every facet of the book's preparation.

To Iris and Morton Manus, who have contributed inestimably toward making this and other books in the Alfred Masterwork series, publications of the finest quality.

To the department heads and staffs of the libraries which have provided us with microfilms and copies of their priceless source materials, so that this edition may be as accurate as it is possible to make it: the Library of Congress, Washington, D.C.; the British Library, London, England; the German State Library, Preussischer Kulturbesitz, Berlin, Germany; the Austrian National Library, Vienna, Austria; the Bergen Public Library, Bergen, Norway; the Library of the Paris Conservatory, Paris, France; and the Robert Schumann Museum, Zwickau, Germany.

Carl Maria von Weber.

WEBER, SCHUBERT, and BEETHOVEN

Carl Maria von Weber, Franz Schubert, and Ludwig van Beethoven are the three most important composers whose works bridge the change in style from classical to romantic.

Carl Maria von Weber (1786-1826) was raised in a theatrical atmosphere, as his father was the director of an itinerant dramatic company. When Abbé Vogler, with whom he studied in Vienna, encouraged him to compose operas, he was well equipped to do so. As Kapellmeister at the Theater in Prague, he was manager, director, administrator, and he also selected the singers. He was able to achieve unprecedented accuracy and unity in the performances of his innovative operas, and he prepared the way for the great operas of Verdi and Wagner.

Even the piano compositions of Weber were often theatrical in color and melody. He was a brilliant virtuoso, and his piano sonatas are technically demanding, full of highly original themes and striking harmonies which were quite new and bold in his time. His eight sets of piano variations are of importance musically and are ingeniously constructed. A short example of one of Weber's variations, based on an aria from an Italian opera, is included on pages 10-13.

A scene from Weber's opera, *Der Freischütz.*

Franz Schubert (1797-1828) was one of the first great composers not dependent on the patronage of either the church or the royal court. He had been thoroughly trained in music at the Royal Chapel in Vienna and had taught for three years in his father's school before his wealthy admirers provided him with financial support that made it possible for him to spend all of his time composing. Thus he was free to create music according to the dictates of his own emotions.

Schubert became especially famous as a composer of songs. He selected his texts from poems that told a story, depicted an emotional situation, or expressed profound human sentiments. His ingenious piano accompaniments created the proper mood for the voice. They not only supported the singer, but helped tell the story by using almost every musical-dramatic means imaginable. Outstanding singers of the day sang these songs at *Schubertiaden* (musical gatherings at which Schubert's compositions were performed) in the homes of Schubert's wealthy friends. The *waltz* was replacing the *menuet* as the most fashionable dance in Europe, and at these parties Schubert often improvised waltzes while his friends danced. Many of these were written down and published in sets, from which any number could be selected and played in succession. One of the most popular of these waltzes is included in this book on pages 14-15.

Schubert also composed church music, symphonies, chamber music, sonatas, and many miniature keyboard works with descriptive titles such as *Moments Musicales, Scherzo, Impromptu,* etc. The *Scherzo* on page 16 is one of his very popular short piano pieces.

Franz Schubert as a young man, when he had already begun to compose songs, symphonies, piano works, etc.

Ludwig van Beethoven's (1770-1827) contributions in breaking the bonds of classicism and ushering in the new romantic era were so monumental that he has been called "the man who freed music." Two of Beethoven's earlier works, composed according to more classical concepts, are found in Alfred's *THE CLASSICAL ERA: An Introduction to the Keyboard Music*. But the confines of classicism were too narrow to contain a musical imagination as inspired as that of Beethoven. His earlier piano sonatas were patterned after those of Haydn, who was one of his teachers, but as he gave more rein to his inspiration, he began to use the form more freely.

The first movement of the *Sonata*, Op. 27, No. 2, is included in this book on page 20. It was subtitled "Moonlight Sonata" by someone other than the composer. Beethoven called this work *Sonata quasi una Fantasia* ("sonata in the style of a fantasy"). By using such a title, he was saying, "This is not in classical form. It expresses what I, Beethoven, feel, and I am free to do this as my genius directs me."

Ludwig van Beethoven.

The performance of only one movement of any of Beethoven's sonatas is perfectly appropriate and in good romantic taste. This was a procedure Beethoven himself suggested to his student, Ferdinand Ries, when Ries performed one of the sonatas in London.

Beethoven composed 32 piano sonatas and many other piano compositions including five concertos. He also composed an opera, many chamber works, orchestral pieces, oratorios, songs, and nine magnificent symphonies.

Beethoven, considered revolutionary by all his contemporaries, lived to be the most respected composer of his day. He had broken precedents, established new ideals of musical expression, and set examples which lesser composers could only strive to equal.

Autograph manuscript of a page from Beethoven's *Sonata quasi una Fantasia*, Op. 27, No. 2, (first movement, measures 14-26). Courtesy of the Beethoven-Haus, Bonn, Germany.

In the first edition of Weber's Variations on the operatic aria *Vień quà Dorina bella*
by Bianchi (facsimile above), the theme appeared as a vocal solo with piano accompaniment.

AIR & VARIATION
Vień quà Dorina bella
(Come here, pretty Dorina)

Theme
Andante M.M. ♩ = 66 - 72

Carl Maria von Weber
Op. 7

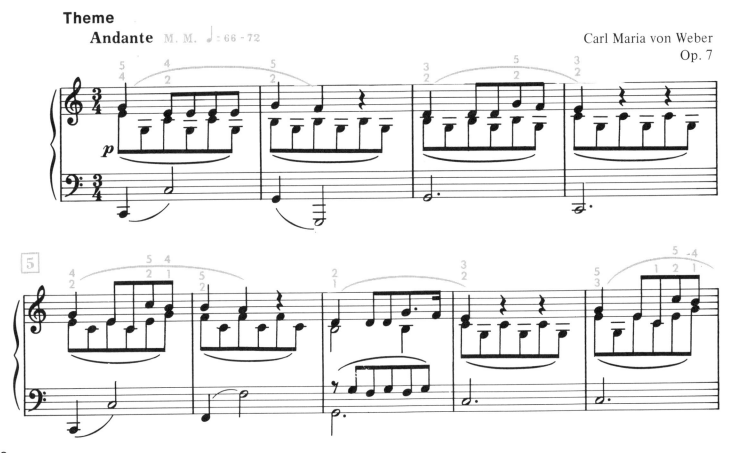

(a) Optional:

(b) During Weber's time, it was customary for a performer to improvise a brief cadenza at fermatas like this. A cadenza such as the following may be played:

(To add a cadenza at measure 16 also would be considered excessive.)

Var. 1

ⓓ The down stem shows that A is the melody note, which must be held. Play the small note and the A together, then release the small note immediately and continue to hold A for its full time value.

A "Schubertiade." Schubert is seated at the piano with the singer, Vogl, beside him. At such gatherings, Schubert improvised waltzes such as the one on this page.
From a painting by Moritz von Schwind.

WALTZ IN B MINOR

Franz Schubert
Op. 18, No. 6

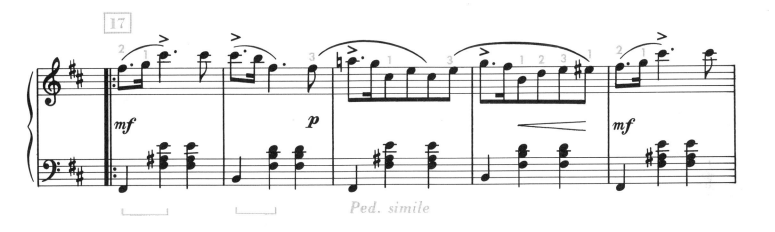

SCHERZO IN B♭ MAJOR

Franz Schubert
D. 593

(a) The appoggiaturas should be played very quickly, on the beat, to emphasize their dissonance.

(b) The repeats, written out in full in the first edition, are not optional with the performer, but should be played. When playing the *da capo*, however, they are omitted, according to traditional style.

senza Ped.

Scherzo da capo
without repeats

SONATA QUASI UNA FANTASIA
"MOONLIGHT SONATA"
dedicated to Countess Giulietto Guicciardi
1st Movement

Ludwig van Beethoven
Op. 27, No. 2

(a) This entire piece must be played very delicately and without dampers (with pedal).

(b) Always very softly and without dampers (with pedal).

For an explanation of the meaning of the two footnotes above, see the discussion under ABOUT PEDALING on page 6.

(c) See the discussion, PROBLEMS IN RHYTHMIC NOTATION on page 6.

(d) The natural before the D is missing in the autograph ms. and the first edition, but is present in later editions.

John Field (1782-1837) was thoroughly grounded in the traditions of the classical school by his father, who was a professional musician, and by Clementi, with whom he studied in London and Paris. However, his piano compositions show that he was not only a completely romantic composer, but also distinctly a forerunner of Chopin. The piano *nocturne* originated with Field. The word comes from the Latin *nocturnus*, meaning "by night." A *nocturne* is a lyrical composition of dreamy or pensive character, appropriate to the evening or night. Fascination with the night and its mysteries is one of the notable traits of the romantic poets, authors, and musicians. Field's use of a flowing bass accompaniment, made of broken chord figures with an elaborately ornamented melodic line was clearly an influence on Chopin. Field was noted for his smooth, even touch at the piano, and his playing was characterized by sensitive dynamics and the most delicate shades of expression.

John Field.

NOCTURNE NO. 5
to Mms. Schimonowsky, St. Petersburg

John Field

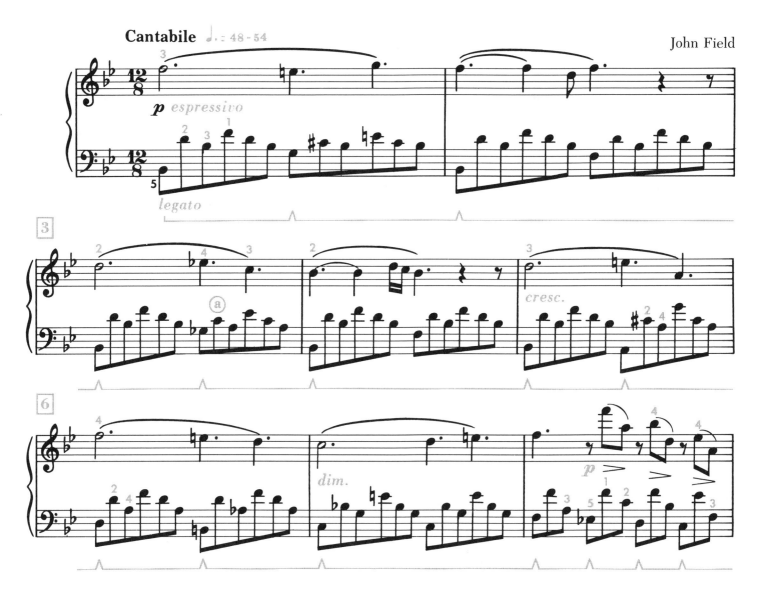

ⓐ The original edition has E instead of C, an engraver's error. See measures 11 & 25.

(b)   Here the turn sign ∾ appears *over* the note; in the reprise (see measure 36) it appears *after* the note. This was probably done deliberately by Field as part of the variation of the reprise. Notice the difference in performance, as indicated in the realizations in light print.

(c)   A diagonal line through the note stem was used by Clementi and others to indicate that the chord should be arpeggiated and an additional, dissonant note added where the line appears. The chord is broken from the bottom upwards, and the notes are sustained except for the dissonant note, **in this case an E♮,** which is released immediately.

ⓓ Here begins the "varied repeat," in the tradition of C. P. E. Bach. This device continued to be used in the romantic period, most notably in the music of Chopin. (See Alfred's *THE CLASSICAL ERA: An Introduction to the Keyboard Music*, pages 11 and 16.)

ⓔ The flexible rhythmic figures in the treble here and in measure 28 are not accommodated rhythms, but TEMPO RUBATO. See the discussion on page 7.

ⓕ In the original edition, the B♭'s in light print do not appear. This could be an engraver's error but might, on the other hand, be a deliberate thinning out of the harmony, to make the F lead more clearly to the G♭ in the following measure.

MENDELSSOHN, SCHUMANN and CHOPIN

Felix Mendelssohn at the age of 11. He had already begun composing for piano and for orchestra.

Felix Mendelssohn (1809-1847) was born into a highly educated family of wealth and position. His great-Aunt Sarah had been the favorite pupil of Wilhelm Friedemann Bach, and his mother was a competent musician who held weekly *soirées* in which the music of Bach was frequently performed. Felix's music teacher, Zelter, took him to visit the aging poet, Goethe, and Mendelssohn introduced Beethoven's works to him by playing his own transcriptions of the symphonies. Mendelssohn's very considerable pianistic talent made him famous at a young age, and his *Overture* to *A Midsummer Night's Dream*, written when he was only 17, firmly established his reputation as a serious composer. Adopting the small, lyrical miniature as a basis for his salon compositions, Mendelssohn used Weber's device of dividing melody between the hands with a broken chord figure accompaniment surrounding it.

Mendelssohn was a leader among those who helped to revive interest in other baroque music. In 1829 he performed Bach's *St. Matthew Passion* with orchestra and chorus in Berlin. This was 100 years after it had been composed, and it had been totally neglected for most of that time. Mendelssohn was also deeply interested in the works of his contemporaries and premiered many of them, including the great *C Major Symphony* of Schubert. Among his friends were most of the leading musicians of his time, including Chopin, Liszt, and Schumann.

Mendelssohn's compositions include symphonies, incidental music for theatrical productions, chamber music, oratorios, songs, a large quantity of salon music, and a number of serious works for piano. His short pieces in song form, called *Songs Without Words*, enjoyed phenomenal success during his lifetime, and many of them are still very frequently performed.

Robert Schumann (1810-1856) began composing when he was only 12 and played the piano with impressive ability. His father was a publisher. The writings of the new romantic poets and novelists, especially Jean Paul, influenced young Robert to write poetry and to develop his literary talents. He studied piano with Friedrich Wieck, whose young daughter Clara was an exceptional pianist. Schumann might have become one of the finest virtuosos, but a device he invented to strengthen his fourth finger ruined his hand and prevented a performing career. Turning instead to composing, Schumann wrote for orchestra, chamber groups, voice, and above all, for piano. His imagination was susceptible to mystic, secret, poetic, and fantastic suggestion, and he filled a dream world with imaginary characters who seemed as real as living people to him.

In 1834 he founded the *Neue Zeitschrift für Musik* (New Magazine for Music), dedicated to criticism, essays, and reviews on music. He wrote under the names of Eusebius, the intellectual; Florestan, the romantic; and Raro, the teacher. He quickly became well known and was recognized as one of the foremost critics of his day. He knew all the leading musicians in Europe and strongly influenced the development and acceptance of the new romantic music. He was one of the first to recognize Chopin's outstanding abilities and to encourage Brahms.

Clara and Robert Schumann.

Schumann married Clara Wieck, who inspired him, nursed him through many illnesses, and cared for him like she would a child during his bouts with the mental disorder that finally ended his life. After his death, she dedicated her life to performing his music, editing his works, and bringing to Schumann the recognition he deserved. Schumann's music is characterized by beautiful, flowing melodies, bold, original harmonies, and an immense amount of imaginative expression.

Schumann's works include one opera, four *symphonies*, six *overtures*, two *piano concertos*, chamber music, instrumental works, vocal solos, duets, and choral works, and many piano compositions including difficult, extended works such as *Carnaval*, *Papillons*, twelve *Symphonic Études*, etc., and some relatively simple works such as *Scenes from Childhood*, which is an album for adults, and *The Album for the Young*, which is a collection for children.

Frederic Chopin, from a famous painting by Eugene Delacroix.

Frederic Chopin (1810-1849) was born the same year as Schumann and one year after Mendelssohn, in a small village near Warsaw, Poland. His father was French, and his mother Polish. He regarded himself as Polish and expressed his intense patriotism by composing many pieces based on Polish national dances, such as the *polonaise* and the *mazurka*, developing these forms beyond any previous concepts of their possibilities.

Chopin's talents as a child prodigy are believed by many to have rivaled those of Mozart. His piano teacher, Adalbert Zywny, and his composition instructor, Josef Elsner, taught him, according to the precepts of C. P. E. Bach, that "ornamentation is indispensable, and the best melodies are poor without it." It is probably for this reason that more ornaments are found in his works than in those of other composers of the romantic era.

When Chopin made his debut in Vienna at the age of 18, the critics praised his delicacy of touch and his great dexterity. But it was Schumann who first opened the eyes of the musical world with his famous lines in the *Neue Zeitschrift für Musik,* "Hats off, gentlemen, a genius!" In 1832 Chopin's debut in Paris made a profound impression on Mendelssohn and Liszt. Liszt performed Chopin's works and made him even more famous, giving them thundering and declamatory interpretations quite different from Chopin's own. Nevertheless, Chopin is said to have remarked to Liszt, "I would like to borrow your way of playing my *Études.*"

Because of his delicate health, Chopin did not concertize extensively but earned his livelihood from his compositions and by teaching wealthy members of the aristocracy. New works by Chopin were eagerly awaited by performers and public, and scarcely a musical gathering took place without the performance of some of his *Waltzes, Nocturnes,* and *Polonaises.* In Chopin's music one finds something so startlingly original that his compositions may be instantly identified. In addition to the brilliance of his music, there is none more lyrical and expressive, and because of this he has earned the title, "poet of the piano." One important characteristic of his playing was his tasteful use of *rubato* (see the discussion on page 7), which was derived from the traditions of Mozart and C. P. E. Bach.

Chopin composed almost exclusively for the piano. His works include two *Concertos*, four *Sonatas* (one for piano & cello), 24 *Études*, 25 *Preludes*, 21 *Nocturnes*, 4 *Scherzos*, 57 *Mazurkas*, 17 *Waltzes*, 16 *Polonaises*, 4 *Ballades*, and many other works such as *impromptus, fantasies, rondos,* other miscellaneous piano pieces, and a few *songs*.

VENETIAN GONDOLA SONG NO. 2
(Venetianisches Gondellied)

Felix Mendelssohn
from *Songs Without Words*
Opus 30, No. 6

(a) The original edition used "rhythmic pedaling," as shown in black print. Many modern pianists prefer the "overlapping pedaling" suggested by the editors (in light print), because of the resonance of the modern piano.

(b) The trills here and in measures 45 and 49 may begin more slowly and gradually accelerate. See the discussion on page 5, # 4.

CONSOLATION

Felix Mendelssohn
from *Songs Without Words*
Opus 30, No. 3

Adagio non troppo M. M. ♩ = 46-50

ⓑ There is no D in this chord in the original edition. This appears to be simply an error in the engraving.

REVERIE
(Träumerei)

Robert Schumann
from *Scenes from Childhood*
Opus 15, No. 7

ⓐ The first edition has ♩ = 100. The Clara Schumann edition has ♩ = 80. Vladimir Horowitz has played it as slow as ♩ = 50.

ⓑ The first edition has only 𝄡 ., as shown in dark print, meaning that the pedal should be used as the performer sees fit. The pedal indications in light print are from the Clara Schumann edition.

ⓒ The first edition has 𝄡 at each of these places, but no release is shown.

The theme occurring in measure 3 and further developed in measures 6, 8, 9, etc., was composed by Schumann's wife Clara and was used in a number of Schumann's compositions. It is often referred to as the "Clara theme." This piece also contains subtle reference to the poet Eichendorff, who was particularly well known for poems about magic forests. A portion of the melody is identical to Schumann's setting of one of Eichendorff's forest poems, in which a lovely bride wanders into the deep woods and falls into the clutches of a witch. Such things as these are frequently found in music of the romantic period, and particularly in that of Robert Schumann.

THE WAYSIDE INN
Herberge

from *Forest Scenes*
Op. 82, No. 6

ⓐ The metronome marking M.M. ♩ = 132, of Clara Schumann, seems much too fast for the indicated moderato tempo.

36 ⓑ Play the small note quickly, *on the beat.*

ⓒ 1st edition: Etwas zurückhaltend.

ⓓ 1st edition: Im tempo.

ⓔ The small note indicates that the trill begins on Bb, *on the beat*. The trill should end, as shown, with a termination. It may have more repercussions, if desired.

(f) 1st edition: Etwas langsamer.

IMPORTANT EVENT
(Wichtige Begebenheit)

Robert Schumann
from *Scenes from Childhood*
Opus 15, No. 6

(a) The first edition has M.M. ♩ = 138. The Clara Schumann edition has ♩ = 120.

(b) The first edition has 𝒫𝑒𝒹. , meaning simply *with pedal*. The Clara Schumann edition has no pedal indications.
The pedaling in light print is by the editors of the present edition.

WALTZ IN A♭ MAJOR
pour M'lle. Marie Wodzińska

Frederic Chopin
Op. 69, No. 1
Posthumous

An autograph copy of this waltz was presented as a farewell gift to Marie Wodzińska, to whom Chopin was once engaged, in September of 1835. It is sometimes called *The Farewell Waltz*. The present edition faithfully reproduces this same autograph, which is now in the National Library at Warsaw. A distinctly different autograph at the Paris Conservatoire is considered to be a less refined version. The posthumous edition of Jules Fontana presents a 3rd version, not substantiated by any known autograph.

(a) Here and in measure 32 the Fontana edition has:

(b) All the ornamental figures such as this one are to be played in *tempo rubato* — see the discussion on page 7. Here the Fontana edition has:

In the final appearance of this section, marked *Da Capo* in the present version, the Fontana edition has:

(c) In measures 13-14 and 38-39 the Fontana edition has:

(d) In the Fontana version the 16th rests in the right hand part in measures 18, 20 and 22 are observed only during the repeat, which is written out in full. The section is marked *con anima*, and the measures are slurred in pairs in measures 17 through 24, the first time the section is played. The left hand part is as follows:

(e) The fingering in dark print is from the autograph manuscript.

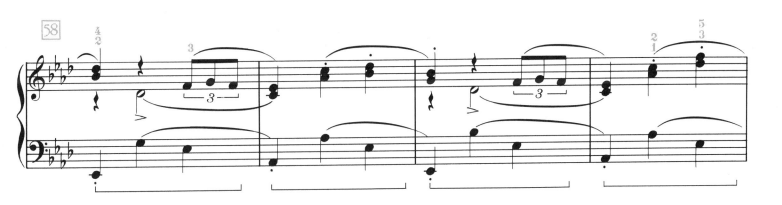

Da Capo al Fine

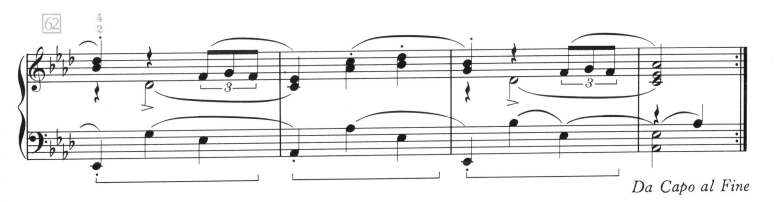

(d) The Fontana version has:

Inspired by the *nocturnes* of John Field (see page 24), Chopin further developed the form into one of the most effective means of romantic expression. Chopin's nocturnes are characterized by a broken-chord accompaniment, and a slow, plaintive melody, embellished with freely flowing decorative figures and arpeggios. See also the discussion of *tempo rubato* on page 7.

NOCTURNE IN C MINOR

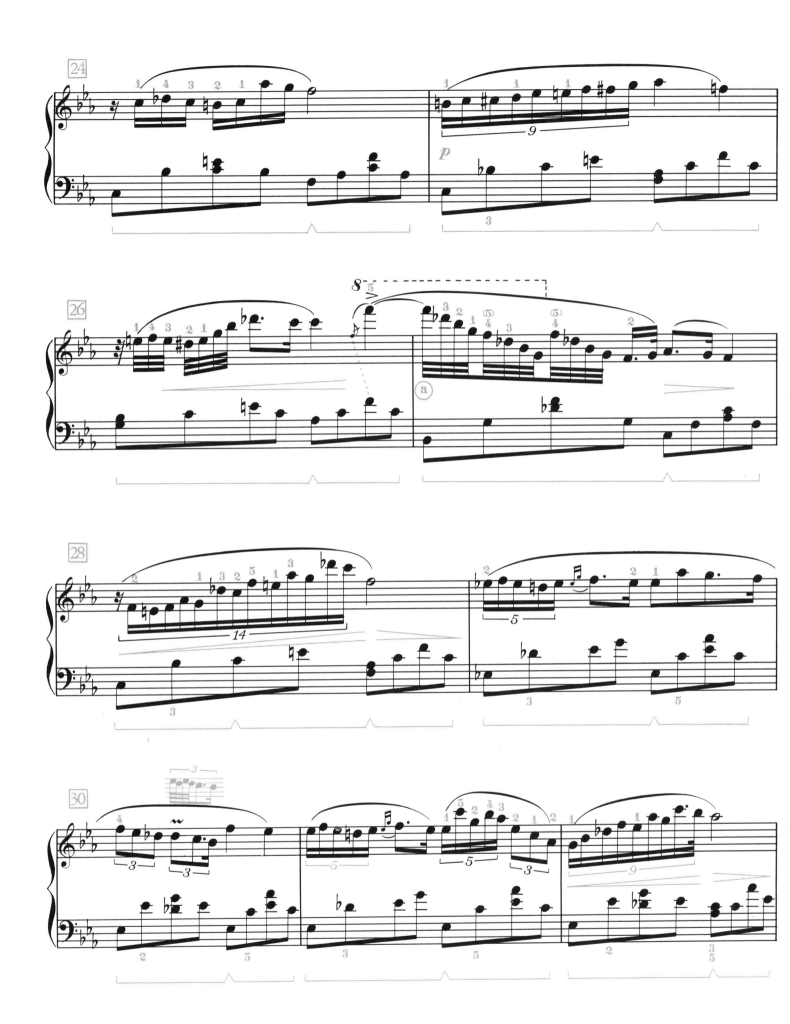

(a) Other editions omit the G in the third group of 32nd notes in this measure, and show the remaining notes as a group of 11 sixteenth notes. Our version is in accordance with the autograph manuscript.

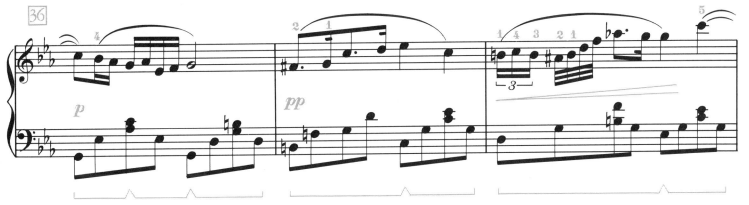

Edvard Grieg (1843-1907) was born in Bergen, Norway. His talent manifested itself when he was a mere child. He was playing the piano by the time he was six, and composing when he was 12. When he was 15, he entered the Leipzig Conservatory, from which he was graduated with distinction. Grieg was admired and praised by most of his contemporaries, including Liszt, Schumann, Brahms, and others. In an interview, Grieg spoke of his own musical style: "Artists like Bach and Beethoven have built churches and temples on the heights. I would like . . . to build dwelling places for my fellow men in which they can feel themselves at home and be happy. In other words, I have recorded my country's folk music. In style and form, I am a German romantic of the Schumann school, but at the same time I have gone to my country's rich treasure of folk tunes, and from this hitherto unexplored wellspring of the Norwegian soul I have tried to create a national art."

Besides many short *Lyrical Pieces* for piano and the celebrated *Concerto in A Minor*, he composed for voice, chorus, and orchestra. His best known orchestral works are the *Peer Gynt* and *Holberg Suites*.

Edvard Grieg as a young man.

WALTZ IN A MINOR

Edvard Grieg
from *Lyric Pieces, Book I*
Opus 12, No. 2

(a) The only complete pedal indication in the Peters printed editions is in measures 78-79. 🞔 is written in measures 1 and 19. The individual pedal indications added editorially in light print are suggestions which the performer may adjust to suit his taste and the resonance of his instrument.

ARIETTA

Poco Andante e sostenuto M.M. ♪ = 84-92

Edvard Grieg
from *Lyric Pieces, Book I*
Opus 12, No. 1

ⓐ Because the two small notes are placed before the bar line, they are played *before the beat* of the following large note.

53

LISZT, BRAHMS, and OTHERS

Franz Liszt was born in 1811, two years after Mendelssohn and only one year after Schumann and Chopin, and he lived to be 75. No better example of the flamboyant, heroic, fantastic side of romanticism can be found than that reflected in the personality, career, abilities, and compositions of this great Hungarian pianist.

Liszt was still a young man when he heard the great violinist, Paganini, perform. Astounded at what Paganini could accomplish with only four strings, Liszt decided that no one had ever approached the full technical possibilities of the piano. He retired from public life for several years to practice. He built his already phenomenal technic to such an extent that the most difficult passages became child's play for him. Nothing was too complicated for him to sight-read perfectly up to the fastest tempo the very first time he saw it. When Grieg was a young man visiting Paris, he showed Liszt his piano concerto, which Liszt read at sight (a little faster than Grieg wanted it performed), all the while commenting to Grieg on the clever ways in which the themes were developed, how it was constructed, and which passages he found particularly beautiful.

Liszt was the first pianist to play a solo recital. With the piano turned sideways so that his handsome profile showed to great advantage, with his head thrown back as if communing with angels, he played with such fantastic technical ability that audiences were overcome. Entering the concert room wearing green gloves, Liszt would slowly remove them and throw them to the ladies, who fought over them. Often while playing, he would gaze at an especially pretty lady until she swooned. Liszt's fame spread throughout Europe, and many Liszt societies were formed. He founded a *National Academy of Music* in his native Hungary and was honored by crowned

"An Evening with Franz Liszt," by the Viennese painter, Joseph Danhauser. Liszt faces a bust of Beethoven. The Countess Marie d'Augolt is seated on the floor beside the piano. Also present, from left to right: Dumas, Hugo, George Sand, Paganini, and Rossini.

heads in many countries. Famous as a teacher as well as a performer, Liszt never accepted money for his teaching, and after 1847 he kept none of the money he received for performing but used all of it to help others.

Liszt's many keyboard compositions include the *Transcendental Études*, *Hungarian Rhapsodies*, and *Variations on a Theme by Paganini*, which are among the most technically difficult piano music ever written. In addition to piano concertos and many transcriptions of orchestral works, he also composed for organ, for solo voices and chorus, and for orchestra. His harmonies foreshadow the works of Debussy, and his development of the one-movement *symphonic tone poem* (for orchestra) influenced Berlioz and many other later composers.

Johannes Brahms (1833-1897) gave his first public piano concert at the age of 14, playing music of Bach and Beethoven and a set of his own variations. He earned his living at first by teaching and playing accompaniments for instrumental soloists, singers, and dancers. In 1853 Schumann wrote in his diary,

"Brahms, a genius, came to see me," and in the October publication of the *Neue Zeitschrift für Musik* he made known to the world the work of this man, whom he believed destined to be a new force in German music.

Brahms as a young man, when he visited the Schumanns in 1853.

The members of the Schumann family became Brahms' closest friends, and both Robert and Clara gave him priceless assistance in his career. Brahms was also influenced by Chopin and Paganini and by the romantic novelist Jean Paul, who inspired virtually all of the romantic composers.

Brahms composed in classical forms and has often been called a *neo-classicist* ("new classicist"), although his music is very romantic in style, using long legato lines and rich harmonies. He was also highly skilled in the use of counterpoint. He was greatly respected by his contemporaries, and his first symphony was hailed as the "Beethoven Tenth." The University at Breslau awarded him a doctorate, and for that occasion he composed the famous *Academic Festival Overture*, using German student-songs as thematic material.

Brahms befriended many young musicians, lending them money, helping them to obtain good positions, and encouraging their writing. Grieg visited him in Vienna, and pleased Brahms with his composing.

Brahms was a virtuoso pianist and wrote little piano music that can be regarded as simple.

Besides the four *symphonies*, he is particularly famous for the *Alto Rhapsody* (for alto, male chorus and orchestra), *A German Requiem* (for soloists, mixed chorus and orchestra), the monumental *Paganini Variations* and *Handel Variations* for piano, two piano concertos, a violin concerto, a double concerto for violin and cello with orchestra, a large number of other vocal and instumental works, and many piano solos. The *waltzes* and *intermezzos* are among the most popular of his piano works.

Brahms as a conductor, around 1890.

Among the host of other romantic composers, there are a few whose contributions to music were outstanding in fields other than piano literature. **Gioacchino Rossini** (1792-1868), Italian opera composer, was the inventor of a new type of comedy set to music. Under the leadership of **Hector Berlioz** (1803-1869), the symphony orchestra was enlarged from the smaller group used in Mozart and Haydn's day to the size of the modern orchestra. But had there been room, Berlioz would have used a thousand musicians, which he actually did in one outdoor concert. **Giuseppi Verdi** (1813-1901), Italian opera composer, used melodramatic plots whose characters seem to be real people. His melodic gifts have made him one of the most popular of all operatic writers.

Richard Wagner (1813-1883) composed a different type of opera, in which the purpose of the music was only to serve the interests of the drama. The orchestra was placed out of sight, so it would not distract from what happened on the stage. He developed the *Leitmotiv*, a short melodic theme identified with each character or situation in the drama, so that the music the orchestra played was more closely united with the action. **Peter Ilich Tschaikovsky** (1840-1893), Russian romanticist, is best known for the ballets *Swan Lake* and *The Nutcracker*. He also composed six symphonies and many miscellaneous compositions for orchestra. Tschaikovsky's piano concertos and violin concerto are among the most frequently performed works in the form. His works include a large number of short piano pieces, including an *Album for the Young*.

You have already seen that most of the great composers of the period composed waltzes for the piano. It was **Johann Strauss, Jr.,** (1825-1899), with his long, lavish, and richly orchestrated compositions (*On the Beautiful Blue Danube, Tales from the Vienna Woods,* etc.), who made the waltz the most popular ballroom dance in Europe.

ADAGIO IN E MAJOR
from FOUR SHORT PIECES

Franz Liszt
from *Four Short Piano Pieces*
(no opus number assigned)

(a) In the autograph and the original edition, the words *Sehr langsam* appear above this piece. These words mean "very slowly" or *adagio*. See also the discussion of TEMPO RUBATO on page 7.

(b) This indication of overlapping pedal was notated 𝄢 𝄢 ❋ by Liszt.

ETUDE IN C MAJOR

(a) Liszt intended to write 48 *etudes* in this opus, two in each major and minor key.

(b) The original tempo indication is ♩ = 132. The speed and brilliance of this piece indicate that TEMPO RUBATO is not appropriate. See the discussion on page 7.

WALTZ IN G♯ MINOR

Johannes Brahms
Opus 39, No. 3

INTERMEZZO IN A MINOR

Johannes Brahms
Op. 76, No. 7